Great Book of Whodunit Puzzles

MEENA

Mini-Mysteries for You to Solve

Falcon Travis

Sterling Publishing Co., Inc.   New York

To Sharon

The characters and situations in this book are entirely imaginary
and bear no relation to any real person or actual happening.

Library of Congress Cataloging-in-Publication Data

Published 1993 by Sterling Publishing Company, Inc.
387 Park Avenue South, New York, N.Y. 10016
Previously published in the United States as
Super Sleuth: Mini-Mysteries for you to Solve
© 1985 by Sterling Publishing Company
Originally published in Great Britain by Knight Books
Text © 1982 by Falcon Travis, illustrations
© 1982 by Hodder & Staughton, Ltd
Distributed in Canada by Sterling Publishing
% Canadian Manda Group, P.O. Box 920, Station U
Toronto, Ontario, Canada M8Z 5P9
Manufactured in the United States of America

Sterling ISBN 0-8069-0348-1

Are You a Super Sleuth?

Find out by trying the puzzles in this book. Here are more than 40 crimes you can solve—thefts, forgeries, break-ins, murders—some of them masterminded by criminals of the highest intelligence (and some by dummies). You'll get the chance to test your powers of deduction on phony alibis, secret codes, and all kinds of baffling evidence. You'll match wits with such law enforcement officers as Luke Sharp, Hans Zupp and Carla Kopp. You'll work on the same cases as the great Inspectors Will Ketchum and Donna DiAnsa.

For some of the mysteries, you'll find extra hints and clues in special sections at the back of the book.

Solutions are at the back of the book, too, but solve the crimes on your own, and you too will be a Super Sleuth!

Contents

Mysteries

1. Three's Company at the Greasy Spoon

Inspector Donna DiAnsa and police informer Stu Pidgeon sat together at a table in the Greasy Spoon Diner. Across the room, three men sat, talking.

"You say those three are known as Slick, Smiley and Mug," said the Inspector, taking out her notebook, "but which is which, Stu? My guess is that the one smoking the cigar is Smiley, the one wearing the hat is Slick, and the one with the mustache is Mug."

"Wrong. All wrong," said Stu.

Just then, the one with the mustache got up from the table. "It's time we took off, Slick," he said. The two got up and all three left, without another word.

"Take another guess," said Stu. "Which one is which?"

"I don't need to guess," Donna DiAnsa said, putting her notebook away, and she correctly named the three men. "Your telling me I guessed all wrong—and those few words from the one with the mustache—was all I needed to put the right labels on them."

Can you correctly label the three men?

Clues on page 103.
Solution on page 109.

2. Art Fake

Artist Kort Fakinnem makes copies of the paintings of popular artists and sells them to crooked dealers, who pass them off as originals. Unfortunately for Kort and for the dealers, Kort usually works from his own rough sketches, using his own imagination (which is not very

good). This leads to careless mistakes that make his fakes fairly easy to detect. In a horse-race picture he copied once, none of the horses had reins for the jockeys to hold onto.

Which of these pictures is the fake? If you have trouble telling, try studying them with a magnifying glass.

Solution on page 109.

3. The Sneak Thief

Inspector Will Ketchum was off duty. He had just arrived at the train station to meet some friends, but their train was running an hour late. As he strolled across the main terminal, a man with the restless eyes of a sneak thief attracted his attention. Then he was lost in a sudden surge of passengers.

A few minutes later, the Inspector spotted the man, who was entering the station's coffee shop. Now he was carrying a leather briefcase. The man sat down at a vacant corner table, placing the briefcase between his chair and the wall.

The Inspector casually followed him in, sat at his table and, identifying himself as a police officer, asked if the man would mind stepping over to the Station Master's office to answer a few questions about the ownership of the briefcase that he had with him. The man claimed indignantly that the briefcase was his, but he agreed to go along.

In the Station Master's office the briefcase lay open on the desk, revealing a file of papers and an envelope containing about $200 in twenty-dollar bills.

"Before we opened this briefcase, Mr. Fink," began the

Inspector, "you told us it was definitely yours and that it contained only a couple of magazines. Now you deny that you are the owner. How do you explain that?"

Mr. Fink rubbed his chin and looked puzzled. "This definitely isn't the briefcase I handed in at the checkroom this morning," he said. "They must have given me someone else's. It looks exactly like mine, but I can see it isn't, now that it's open. My briefcase was locked and all it had in it were some magazines I was reading on the train. The owner of this briefcase shouldn't have left it open with all this money in it. If he got mine by mistake, he isn't going to be very happy about it."

"I'm sure he won't be," said the Inspector. "What is more, he's probably wondering, as I am, why anyone would check a briefcase that had only a couple of magazines in it."

"That's easy to explain," said Mr. Fink. "I got to town this morning just before noon on one of those one-day round-trip excursion tickets—and I'll be going back tonight—if you don't make me miss my train. I was reading the magazines on the train. I brought my briefcase because I was hoping to find some secondhand books, but I didn't get to the bookstores because I met an old friend who invited me over to his house."

"So that's when you checked your briefcase?"

"That's right," continued Mr. Fink. "I didn't want to carry it around with me, so I left it here and went to visit with my friend. Got my taxi fare paid both ways, had a great time and all I had to spend since I got off the train this morning was what they charged me at the checkroom."

"Lucky you," said the Inspector. "Now would you mind emptying out all your pockets and placing their contents on this desk?"

"I don't mind at all," said Mr. Fink, "I've got nothing to hide. The sooner you're satisfied, the sooner I can get

going. I have to take this briefcase back to the check-room and see if mine is still there."

Mr. Fink's statement and the contents of his pockets (shown above) were enough to tell Will Ketchum whether or not the suspect was telling the truth. If you have decided, too, turn to the Solutions Section and see if you reached the same conclusion as the Inspector, and for the same reasons.

If you haven't been able to decide yet, turn to the Clues Section for some pointers to the clues that helped the Inspector make up his mind.

Clues on page 103.
Solution on page 109.

4. Odd Man Out

"I've been robbed," said Mr. E. Z. Mark when he called in at the main police station of the resort town. "Someone took my wallet while I was standing with my wife, my daughter and our dog in front of the gift shop on Main Street."

"Did you notice anything suspicious?" asked Detective Sue Smart.

"Well, while we were looking in the window," Mark said, "another family came along—a man and a woman and a young girl and their dog. I didn't take much notice of them at the time. Then one of those street photographers called out to us and snapped a picture. Maybe he thought we were all together. But we didn't want to order any photos, and we went on to lunch."

"When did you first miss your wallet?" asked the Detective.

"As soon as I went to pay the bill at the restaurant," said Mr. Mark. "Luckily, my wife had some money with her. And as we walked back to the hotel, we passed the photographer's stand, noticed our photo in their display frame and bought it. We expected to see six people on it, but there are seven." He took the photo from his pocket and handed it to the Detective.

"Which is the person who wasn't with your family or the other three people?" asked the Detective.

"I don't know," answered Mr. Mark. "I hardly looked at any of them."

The Detective took down all the details, asked Mr. Mark to leave the photo and call back in a few days. Then she took the photo to Detective Noah Tall, who had just taken a training course for detectives.

"Here's something to test your skill," she told Detective Tall. "This mixed-up group consists of two separate families: each one made up of man, woman, child and dog. The extra man is probably the pickpocket. Can you put together the families and tell me which one is the 'odd' man?"

Noah Tall did it, calling the groups Family A and Family B. Can you figure it out?

Clues on page 103.
Solution on page 110.

5. Doggone Kids

Farmer Jones was complaining to officer Luke Sharp about four boys from town who had trespassed on his land and let their dogs run loose among his chickens.

"The collie and the pug did damage that the boys' folks ought to pay for," said the farmer. "But the dogs weren't on leashes, and the boys ran away when they saw me coming, so I don't know which dog belonged to which boy."

"What about the other dogs?" asked Officer Sharp.

"There was a boxer and an Irish setter," said the farmer. "Two of my workmen saw the boys before. They nicknamed 'em Red, Scruffy, Shorty and Curly. They said they saw Shorty and Red out with the boxer and the pug one time. And later they saw Scruffy and Curly with the collie and the Irish setter. They once saw the collie and the pug with Curly and Shorty, too."

"That information," said Officer Sharp, "is enough to tell me which dog belongs to which boy. Come into town tomorrow and we'll go over to the high school. If you can point out the boys, I'll question the two whose dogs did the damage."

Which dog belonged to which boy?

Clues on page 103.
Solution on page 110.

6. Meanwhile Back
at the Hideout . . .

Found—an envelope containing six small pieces of paper. It was lying on the floor of the deserted hideout of Crypto, the sinister crime organization. Written on each piece was a group of words and a number.

Under the flap of the envelope was a note, which read:

"Arrange these pieces in pairs, in the number order you've been given, and read it like a book."

The detective who found the envelope arranged the pieces in numerical order—1–6, as shown on the opposite page.

While he tried out various arrangements of the pieces, his colleague copied the words out on six bits of paper, and between them they found the correct order and the meaning of the message. Can you?

Solution on page 111.

7. Counterfeiting Ring

Will Ketchum settled into his chair as Sergeant Zupp came into his office. "Have all three arrived, Hans?" he asked.

Sergeant Zupp nodded. "They all agreed to come and answer a few questions. The storeowner objected at first, but the cab driver and the painter were willing enough."

Inspector Ketchum looked pleased. "If one of them is passing the counterfeit bills around, this could be our first real lead in this case. I'll talk to them all together. I've read their statements so far. Tell them to come in."

The Sergeant brought the men in and introduced them as Mr. Sales the storeowner, Mr. Brush the painter and Mr. Haack the cabdriver.

"Gentlemen," said the Inspector, when all were seated, "the bank informs us that they found four counterfeit dollar bills among the cash deposited by Mr. Sales last Wednesday. They were easy to spot because they were all new bills and they all had the same number on them. Mr. Sales, you say four new bills and one old one were handed to you by Mr. Brush that morning—and those singles were the only new bills among the cash you deposited?"

"Correct," said Mr. Sales. "I might have noticed there

was something unusual a▚
over the counting of the day's▚
answered a phone call from a bus▚

"Mr. Brush," said the Inspector, "yo▚
had any counterfeit bills in your possessio▚
have gotten them in your change from the cab▚

"Must have," answered the painter. "They looked ▚
to me when I paid for the groceries. But I only had six
dollars on me—a five-dollar bill and a single. I handed
the driver the five-dollar bill—I remember—because I'd
jotted down a telephone number on it that I didn't want
to forget. The next time I spent any money was in
Sales's store and then all I had left was some loose
change till the bank opened."

Inspector Ketchum turned to the cabdriver. "Mr.
Haack, you say you don't remember much about Mr.
Brush's trip from the station because you were running
late and had to stop for gas before you could meet the
next train. But Mr. Brush didn't see your tank being
filled."

"Of course not," said the cabdriver. "I just got a few
dollars worth at a self service station right after I
dropped him off, and I made up for lost time."

"Thanks for your time, gentlemen," said Inspector
Ketchum, "I may be grateful for it later on."

After the Sergeant showed the three men out, Inspector Ketchum handed him a slip of paper with a name
written on it. "That man was lying, Hans," he said.
"Keep an eye on him."

Whose name did the Inspector write down?

Clues on page 104.
Solution on page 111.

...out them if I hadn't handed ...take to my wife while I ...ess friend." ...say that if you ...you must ...driver?"...

O̶.̶ was the first on the scene of the accident. ̶car had overturned in a dry ditch. Nobody was ̶ ̶sly hurt, but all five occupants were badly shaken up.

"Who was driving, Luke?" asked Detective Sue Smart as soon as she arrived.

"Don't know yet," said Luke, very confused. "I've only just managed to get any sense out of two of them, so far. The two fellows and girls picked up a hitchhiker, so there were three of them sitting in the back seat and two in the front. The hitchhiker says he was sitting next to the blonde, and the girl with the brown hair was sitting next to someone she calls Jim."

He looked down at his notes and went on, "The girl named Pam said she was sitting next to the hitchhiker, and Ann was sitting next to Ben. That's all the information I've got."

"It's enough to tell me who was driving," said the detective.

Who was driving?

Clues on page 104.
Solution on page 111.

9. Lying in the Gym

The window in the school gym had been broken and, since none of the four boys present at the time would admit who did it, the gym teacher had them up before the principal.

"Who broke the window?" asked the principal.

Said Tim: "It wasn't me, sir."

Said Tom: "It was Dan, sir."

Said Dan: "It was Tim, sir."

Said Don: "No, it wasn't."

"I know boys well enough to know when they're telling the truth," said the principal, "and I'm sure that only one of you has just told the truth. That also tells me which one of you broke the window."

The principal was right: Only one boy was telling the truth. Which one broke the window?

Clues on page 104.
Solution on page 111.

10. Cracked!

"So this is the scene of the gun battle, Sergeant," said Inspector Donna DiAnsa, standing outside the shop whose window and glass doors were cracked by bullets.

"Hardly a battle," said Sergeant Hugh Dunitz. "Only one side was armed. The two in the hospital are members of the Slobbo Gang. They were walking past this shop when a car came alongside and two men opened fire on them with handguns."

"Thanks for bringing me up to date, Sergeant," said the Inspector. "This would happen while I was off duty. What about the gunmen?"

"There were plenty of witnesses," said the Sergeant. "They've been identified as Potsy Segal and Fuzzy Morgan of the Moron mob."

"They'll be lying low, I imagine," said the Inspector, "but we know where to look for them. In the meantime, make a sketch of the cracks in these two glass doors and the window, showing how they run from each bullet hole. I want to take a closer look at the holes. I'd bet that one of the guns was of a bigger caliber than the other."

Back at headquarters, Inspector DiAnsa and Sergeant Dunitz studied the statements of the witnesses and notes they made at the scene.

"According to the witnesses," said the Sergeant, "the shooting started as the two Slobbos were passing the glass doors. One Slobbo—"Legs"—made for the doorway, and the other one—"Ears"—went on past the window. Legs was hit when he was in the doorway, Ears was hit in front of the window. As you can see in my sketch, one of the glass doors got two bullets through it; the other got three, and the window got four."

The Inspector nodded in agreement. "We know that the two weapons were of different calibers, that they made different sounds and slightly different-sized holes, and we know Potsy likes a bigger caliber gun. We also know that the gun that put the second hole in the door

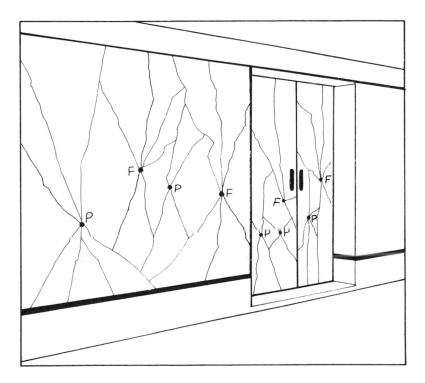

fired the shot that hit Legs. And the gun that put the third hole in the window fired the shot that hit Ears."

"Looking at my sketch," said the Sergeant, "we can figure out which bullet hole was the second one in the door, because a crack stops when it reaches a crack that's already there."

"Right" said the Inspector. "A stopped crack is a later crack than the one that stops it. I've marked the bigger caliber holes with P for Potsy and the others with F for Fuzzy. I'll leave it to you to figure out who shot Legs and who shot Ears."

Can you figure it out?

Solution on page 112.

11. The Crypto Caper

Sergeant Zupp came into Inspector Ketchum's office and handed him a sheet of paper.

"We took this from one of the members of Crypto,"

```
O2  342DAY  A5  3I9  6E5  57E  6A26

506E57ER  A5  57E  842IPER  5REE

I22  50  PLA2  04R  2E95  8I6  8OB
```

said the Sergeant. "We have him in the next room. His boss likes using secret codes. It's too soon to make any sense out of it, but it doesn't look as if it's going to be too much of a problem. Only eight letters of the alphabet seem to be in code; the rest are left unchanged. Instead of the eight letters, they've used eight figures from 2 to 9. I suppose they didn't use the figures 1 and 0 because they didn't want them to get mixed up with the letters I and O."

"Strictly speaking," said Will Ketchum, "this is a cipher. That short code-breaking course we had to take—because of Crypto's activities—has helped us to put most of them behind bars." He took a scrap of paper, copied the message out, and handed the original back to the Sergeant. "Return this to the suspect," he said, "looking as puzzled as you can, and let him go. His boss still thinks we're too dumb to break his codes. This one won't take long."

Can you decipher the message?

Clues on page 104.
Solution on page 112.

12. Down at the Dirty Duck

When Nita Bath the waitress at the Dirty Duck Restaurant brought Detective Sergeant Hans Zupp his usual cup of coffee, she had something special to tell him.

"Those three fellows at the far table are up to something," Nita whispered. "I saw one of them slip a revolver to one of the others he called Eddie. By their accents, I'd say they're all foreign. One of them's English, one's an Australian and I think the other one is French."

"Which is which?" asked the Detective.

"The one on Eddie's right is the Australian, and the Frenchman is on the Englishman's right."

"Which one is Eddie?" asked the Detective, but Nita was called away before she could answer, and the three men were getting up to leave.

The detective followed the men outside, made an excuse to get them into conversation and—having already worked out for himself what Eddie's nationality was—soon discovered who was carrying the gun.

Which one was Eddie?

Clues on page 104.
Solution on page 112.

13. Alibis

Inspector Ketchum and Sergeant Zupp walked into the poolroom where, as they suspected, the men they were looking for were spending their time. The three had grouped their chairs into a circle in a corner of the room and were talking quietly. The talking stopped as the plainclothes detectives approached.

"May we join you for a few minutes, Jack?" said the Inspector.

"We're not fussy about the company we keep," grinned Jack Cass. "This is Cluck on my right, and Deke on my left."

"They know us well enough," growled Cluck, as the detectives drew up a couple of chairs and joined the group.

"We're making inquiries about a break-in at Bradlaw's factory last week," began the Inspector. "A skillful job. The kind of job that makes me think of you three."

Jack laughed. "You flatter us. But if it was last week, why didn't you come around before?"

"Because the factory has been closed for vacation and they just discovered the open safe this morning," explained the Inspector.

"What day are we talking about, Inspector?" asked Jack. "The only nights last week that I can prove what I was doing are Monday and Wednesday. On Wednesdays I'm always in here. And last Monday my wife dragged me to a show with her mother. I don't like spending the money, but it was my mother-in-law's fiftieth birthday. Never again. It was a waste of good money. I gave the guy at the box office a hundred dollar bill for those tickets and didn't even get a penny of change. It was highway robbery."

"You don't say," said the Inspector.

"Correct," said Jack. "I can tell you anything you'd like to know about the show. If you want proof, I've got the ticket stubs at home."

"I don't have any more questions right now, Jack," said the Inspector. "It was Monday night that we think the break-in took place, because some lights were seen at the factory that night, but they weren't reported until too late." He turned to Deke. "Where were you last Monday?"

"It's a funny thing," said Deke, "but my wife and my daughter and I went to the same theatre as Jack that night. Great minds think alike, I guess. But we sat in cheaper seats. I haven't got any stubs to prove I went, but one of the ushers will probably remember the mixup we had over our seats. Our seat numbers were Row M-3–4 and 5, but there were three old ladies sitting in them and they didn't want to move. Anyway, an usher got them to move up to seats 6, 7 and 8."

"You think an usher would remember that?" asked Sergeant Zupp.

"Maybe not," said Deke, "but there was a big fuss during the second act when I lit a cigarette. A kid sitting next to me told me smoking wasn't allowed. I told her parents that were sitting beside her to keep their rotten brat at home next time. They'll remember me, even if the usher doesn't."

Inspector Ketchum smiled and asked Cluck whether he had gone to the theatre that Monday night, too.

"No," answered Cluck. "I was home all evening. I watched TV till the end of the 11 o'clock news. Then I covered the canary, let the dog in, put the cat out, fed the piranha, checked to make sure the windows and doors were locked, put out the lights and went to bed. And I can't prove any of it."

"Thank you for your cooperation, gentlemen," said Inspector Ketchum, getting up, "but I'm afraid a few more questions are called for. Sergeant Zupp and I are going back to the station, but not alone."

Who accompanied the detectives back to the station?

Clues on page 104.
Solution on page 112.

14. Post Office

Three men took part in a robbery of the post office, and they were arrested later while abandoning the stolen car they used.

They had worn face masks, but witnesses had noted some useful details, such as height and hair color, as well as the names they called each other and the part each one played in the holdup. The details were sketchy, but good enough for the detective in charge of the case to piece together a rough description of each one: name, height, hair color, and which one was the driver, the lookout and the gunman. Can you do the same?

Here is what the witnesses said:

1. The gunman was shorter than the lookout.
2. The one called Jim was shorter than the driver.
3. Jim was taller than the redheaded man.
4. Mush was taller than the dark-haired man.
5. Tim was shorter than the blond.

Clues on page 104.
Solution on page 113.

15. Under Surveillance

The police have Swifty Moran under observation. A police photographer set up his camera in a neighboring building that looked out over Swifty's garage, and he took a series of photos, which can be seen on the opposite page.

Unfortunately, the processors sent the photos back in the wrong sequence. Can you put them in the right order?

Solution on page 113.

16. The Coin Expert

Inspector Donna DiAnsa and Sergeant Dunitz turned into a narrow side street and headed toward the little shop of C. J. Silver, buyer and seller of coins and medals. They stood in front of the shop for a few minutes, studying the trays of coins on display. Then, after briefly consulting an inventory of stolen property, the Inspector put the list into her purse and went to the door. As she turned the handle, a young man came to the door and unbolted it.

"You're opening late this morning," said the Inspector, as she walked inside, followed by Sergeant Dunitz. "Is Mr. Silver in?"

"Mr. Silver is my uncle. I'm helping him as much as I can until he can get around again," explained the young man. "He hurt his foot badly a few days ago, but he comes in every day anyway. I couldn't manage this place if he didn't. I don't know anything about coins. He's in his workroom at the back, sorting out a batch of coins. I've just been making us some coffee."

"We know your Uncle George very well," said Inspector DiAnsa. "We're police officers. Sorry to hear about his accident. Our questions won't keep you long. Your uncle is one of the great authorities on rare coins. His own private collection is worth a fortune, as I'm sure you know. I remember him telling me that as an only child and a lifelong bachelor, he's used to being on his own and really prefers his own company, but I'm sure he's glad to have you around at a time like this."

"I hope so," said the young man. "I'm doing my best. Now how can I help you? I hope Uncle hasn't been breaking the law."

"No, nothing like that," said the Inspector. "It's a general query about Roman coins. It cropped up the other day at the station, and I'd like to be sure about it. Will you go ask your uncle whether the date on an early Roman coin has the B.C. in front of it or after it? For example, B.C. 55 or 55 B.C.? I think 55 B.C. is correct."

The young man disappeared into the back of the store and Inspector DiAnsa turned to the Sergeant. "The man's a fraud, Hugh," she said. "When he comes back out here with the answer, if I put my hand up on the counter, grab the man and hold him. Otherwise, leave the next move to me. The real business we came about can wait."

"You were right, Officer," said the man, as he came back into the room, "55 B.C. is correct."

Inspector DiAnsa put her hand on the counter. Sergeant Dunitz grabbed the man in a vise-like hold. The Inspector dashed through to the back room and found Mr. Silver lying bound and gagged and in a dazed state.

"How did you know that fellow was a fraud?" asked Mr. Silver later, after a police van had taken the man away.

"He made three slips, Mr. Silver," answered Donna DiAnsa. "Or rather, I led him into making three slips."

"I spotted two of them," said Sergeant Dunitz.

How many did you spot?

Clues on page 104.
Solution on page 113.

17. More Doggone Kids

Remember the four boys who trespassed on Farmer Jones's land with their dogs? Well, they weren't the only ones.

"I'm getting tired of you kids letting your dogs run loose on my land," the farmer said. "This black one would have got itself shot t'other day, if I'd had my gun with me. Which one of you does it belong to?"

The redheaded girl looked at the girl with the braids, and the skinny girl looked at the freckled-faced girl, but nobody answered.

"I know which dog belongs to which girl," said Tom, the farmer's son, who came racing up the road, and he correctly paired each dog with its owner.

The farmer sent the girls and their dogs on their way with a warning. Then, turning to Tom, he asked how he came to know which dog belonged to which girl.

"I've never spoken to those kids—or to anyone who knows them," said Tom, "but I've seen them around." He went on to explain, "Last Monday I saw Red, Braids and Freckles with the German shepherd and the poodle. On Friday, I saw Skinny, Braids and Red with the cocker spaniel and the German shepherd. Then yesterday in the village, I saw Freckles and Red with the poodle. That's how I know which dog belongs to which girl, and which girl doesn't have a dog."

Do you know?

Solution on page 114.

18. Cliff Tragedy

John Fell was found dead at the foot of Eagle Rock during a camping trip. His three companions made statements to the police.

Said Bill Brewer: "I was in my tent reading when the others went out. Too bad about John. He shouldn't have come with us. I never paid any attention to his boasting and his sarcasm, but it caused some pretty sore feelings between him and Harry and Peter."

Said Harry Hawk: "We were going along the cliff top. John found a coil of rope. He tied one end around a tree and dared Peter and me to lower ourselves down to one of the ledges. He called us chicken because we wouldn't do it. When we left him, he was tying the rope around his own waist."

Said Peter Price: "When Harry and I left John, we lost sight of him right away because of the bushes along the edge of the cliff. Before we got to the beach path, we heard a sort of a scream. We ran back to where we'd left John. Part of the rope was still tied to the tree. We looked over the edge of the cliff and there was John, lying on the deserted beach. While Harry ran down to him, I went to the Collins farm. They phoned the police."

"Does this seem like a simple accident to you, Sergeant?" asked Inspector Keith Smilen.

"Not really, Inspector," said the Sergeant. "It looks like murder to me. Look at the clean-cut end of that rope. The end of the rope that's fastened to the tree looks exactly the same. Somebody must have cut it."

"Think again, Sergeant," said the Inspector. "And look again. You missed seeing something that tells a different story about the use of the rope."

What is wrong with the Sergeant's theory?

Solution on page 114.

19. The Protection Racket

The gang of four that once ran the biggest protection racket in the east eventually got out of jail. Almost immediately, they began operating again in the same neighborhood. They had previously divided it into four territories: north, south, east and west. Because each mobster had always kept his operations in the same area, the police nicknamed them Mr. North, Mr. South, Mr. East and Mr. West.

Now the police received a reliable tip that this time each mobster was operating in a new territory. None of the new victims was willing to identify the mobsters from photos the police showed them, but three facts became clear, and that was enough for the FBI to work out which mobster was operating where. These are the facts.

1. Mr. East is not operating the North.
2. The North territory is not being operated by Mr. South.
3. The South territory is not being operated by Mr. East.

Can you tell who is operating in each territory?

Solution on page 114.

20. The Braney Safe

The home of the inventor Professor Braney had been broken into, and Detective Sue Smart went to investigate.

"There are two safes," said the Professor. "They must have guessed the combination of the one they opened, but the other one seemed to baffle them. Both the combinations were in numbers when I bought the safes, but I forget numbers and when I write them down I lose the pieces of paper they're written on. So I changed the figures to letters and arranged them in words I could remember."

"Numbers are more secure than words," said Detective Smart. "Words can be guessed, but not numbers." She walked over to the first safe. "How does this four-dial combination work?"

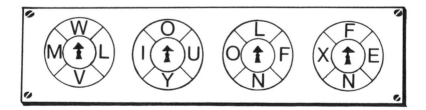

"You have to turn the knobs so that the arrows point to the letters that spell the secret word. Read across from left to right," the Professor said.

"Ingenious," said the Detective.

"But that's not all," said Professor Braney. "The ends of the arrows also must point to the letters of another secret word. Try it. I'll give you a clue. The two words are wild animals. As the dials are set right now, the arrow-heads spell WOLF, but the arrow-ends spell VYNN, which isn't an animal, so the safe stays locked."

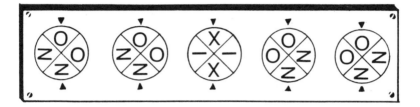

After a few minutes, Detective Smart found the correct combination, which convinced the Professor that he'd better change the combination back to numbers.

"Try the one that baffled the burglars," said the Professor. "This is a five-dial combination. When it is set to open, the letters across the top, from left to right, spell a common word; and the letters across the bottom, from right to left, spell the same word. I admit this is tricky, but that's why it fooled the burglars. I remember the word because I like the taste of this."

Detective Smart grinned. "The taste of zoxox?"

Can you discover the combination words?

Solution on page 115.

21. The Card Players

Sergeant Hans Zupp and police informer Stu Pidgeon made their way down Dead End Alley toward the Quick Shuffle Club.

"So this is where the gang meets to discuss their jobs," said Sergeant Zupp. "I'd like a look inside."

They passed the door and stopped outside a low, streaked window.

"See those four who are playing cards?" whispered Stu. "They are Doc, Fingers, Kinky and Spider. Kinky's the boss. That's Fingers with his back to us."

"Kinky's the one I'm most interested in," said Sergeant Zupp. "Is that him sitting opposite Fingers?"

"No," answered Stu, "he's on Spider's left."

"Thanks, Stu," said Sergeant Zupp, "Let's go. Someone's coming this way."

"But I've only told you which one is Fingers," protested Stu. "We'd better come back when the coast is clear."

"No need," said Hans Zupp, moving off. "I don't need any more information to be able to put a name to all four."

Can you name them correctly, clockwise, from Fingers on?

Solution on page 115.

22. The Clickspring Caper

While Inspector Will Ketchum was on vacation, he liked to sit with his hound dog Sherlock at his feet, and talk with the local police Sergeant at the local hotel. One day a farmhand burst in and called urgently to a man at the next table:

"Mr. Paley!" he shouted, "they broke into the mansion! They got in through a side window and it's wide open and so is the front door. You're to get back there as fast as you can! Officer Sharp sent me—he's waiting there with Tom Bean. He found him on the grounds with a bag of stuff from the house. Tom says the thief must have dropped it!"

Sergeant Mull turned to Will Ketchum as Mr. Paley hurried out. "Want to come along to the mansion, Will? It's only a couple of hundred yards up the road. My car's outside."

In the car, the Sergeant explained that the owners of the mansion, Mr. and Mrs. Clickspring, were away on a safari, and the only one living in the house was Mr. Paley, the caretaker. Tom Bean was a handyman who also did some gardening around the place when the Clicksprings were home. When they were away—as they were now—they left a key at the police station, and Mr. Paley had the only other key.

The Sergeant drove his car up the winding drive and they stepped out at the open front door of the mansion, where Tom Bean and Mr. Paley were standing with Officer Sharp, who was holding a bulky sack.

Sergeant Mull introduced Will Ketchum, listened to Sharp's account, and then turned his attention to Tom Bean.

"What's your story, Mr. Bean?" asked the Sergeant.

"About ten o'clock this morning," Bean said, "I was riding past the gates when I noticed that a ground floor window of the mansion was open. It looked as if the glass was broken. So I came to see."

"And what did you find?"

"Come around to the side window and I'll show you."

They all followed Tom Bean along a paved path close beside the house and stopped outside a ground floor window that was wide open with a hole in the glass where the lock was. In the soft earth below the window was a pair of heavy footprints, toes pointing toward the wall. Broken glass was scattered around, some of it pressed firmly into the ground, as if by the heavy tread.

"This is what I found," said Bean. "I'm no detective, but it looked to me as if the thief stood here, broke the glass, undid the catch, pushed the window up and then climbed inside. I thought he might still be in there, so I decided to run over to the police station, but when I passed the corner of the mansion, I noticed that the front door was open."   .

"What then?" asked Sergeant Mull.

"I thought the thief must have heard me and ran out through the front door," continued Bean, "and that maybe Mr. Paley was inside—tied up or hurt. So I went inside, calling and looking for him. In this room—with the broken window—I found the sack that the thief must have dropped. I picked it up and then I heard loud footsteps from the direction of the gate. I couldn't see who it was from the window because of the trees. I thought it might be the thief coming back, so I ran outside and made for the woods. It was officer Sharp, and he spotted me and thought I was the thief. I think he still does."

"Big footprints. . . . Has anyone seen footprints like these before?" asked the Sergeant.

"It's about the size Mr. Clickspring takes," said Mr. Paley. "It looks like the shoes he wears when he putters around in the garden. He keeps a few old pairs in the garden shed. He sometimes gives away old boots to people who come around doing odd jobs like chopping wood, and to vagrants that come by."

The Sergeant turned to Officer Sharp. "I'll leave you to make a sketch of these prints. And after you've checked the contents of the sack with Mr. Paley, have a look around the grounds. I'll take Inspector Ketchum back to the hotel and join you later."

On the way back in the car, Sergeant Mull commented on Inspector Ketchum's silence.

"I don't interfere in what isn't my business, John," said the Inspector, "but since you're asking for my opinion, it's brief. You don't need to look around for any big-footed tramp."

Who then?

Clue on page 105.
Solution on page 115.

23. Art Fake Two

Which of these pictures is Kort Fakinnem's copy—and which is the original? Remember, if you have trouble telling, check with a magnifying glass.

Solution on page 116.

24. The Forgers

The police thought the forgers were operating from three trailer trucks that were standing side by side on the Crary farm. One man occupied each truck, and the farmer knew them only as Tom, Dick and Harry. The police had reason to believe they were printing twenty-dollar bills—and larger—and that one man was the engraver, one the printer, and the third the distributor, who stocked the newly printed bills in his truck.

"We haven't been able to pick up much information about this bunch," said Officer Sharp to Sergeant Mull, "but I think the few bits of conversation we've overheard—and what we've observed through binoculars—is as much as we need to tell us who occupies each truck and what part he plays in the organization."

"Carry on, Luke," said the Sergeant.

"We're sure," continued Luke Sharp, "that the man they call Harry isn't the one next to the printer, as we first thought. As seen through the binoculars, Harry is on the right of Tom, and Dick is next to the engraver. So that means—"

"Let me work it out for myself," interrupted Sergeant Mull, which he soon did. Can you?

Solution on page 116.

25. Crypto Strikes Again

"What do you make of this, Sergeant?" asked Detective Smart. She handed him a folded sheet of paper. "I was questioning a suspect about a stolen car that he said he had just bought secondhand. This fell out of his wallet while he was looking for the receipt."

"A receipt he couldn't find, I bet," said Sergeant Zupp. The detective nodded.

The Sergeant examined the sheet of paper. "This is almost certainly a Crypto communication. It could be important. So could your suspect. The brains behind the organization doesn't trust telephones, so the top boys pass coded messages when they're planning something big. Where is the suspect and what did he have to say about this?"

"He's in the station house," said Sue Smart. "He says he must have picked up the piece of paper at home, by mistake. It belongs to his son, who's a Boy Scout."

"Get me a copy of it," said the Sergeant. "Then he can have it back with our compliments. This code is made up of typewriter symbols. And by the look of it, your man has already begun to decode it. You must have interrupted him. He only got as far as the first word and

Line 1:
% = ? $ @   ? & $ ⊬ * " $ + :
A F TE R   T   E   T

Line 2:
≠ % @ % ⊬ $ ($ ⊬ $ " $ @ ⊬
A R A   E   E   E   E R

Line 3:
! & + ⊬   (+ −   ? & $! & % @ $
T   E   A R E

Line 4:
+ ◊ ?   ⊬ * " " "   − $ % ?   ? & $
T   E   AT   T   E

Line 5:
= *) $ (+ " " ⊬   ! % * " + @ !
F   E   A   R

Line 6:
? %) $ @ :   ? $ " "   : ◊ ? ? ⊬
TA   E R   TE   T T

Line 7:
% : ⊬ % "   ? +   − $? & $ @ $
A   A   T   E T   E R E

filled in the same letters throughout the message. Inspector Ketchum will be back in a couple of minutes. So far he's broken all their codes. And Crypto thinks they're unbreakable."

Here's what the code looked like:

When Inspector Ketchum returned, he went to work on the secret message. Detective Smart kept the suspect talking until Ketchum was finished. Then the man was allowed to leave, but he was followed. What did the message say?

Solution on page 117.

26. The Bank Robbery

Four cars were going to be used in the bank robbery.
"Now, remember," the boss said, "until you get to Red
Water Junction, you've got to travel in the order I just
told you. What's the order, Lem?"

LEM: First the Chevy, then the Datsun, the Ford and
the Toyota.

BOSS: You got only two right. Tell him, Clem.

CLEM: The Ford, the Toyota, the Datsun and the
Chevy.

BOSS: Only one right. One that Lem got wrong.
Now, you, Mutt.

MUTT: Chevy, Toyota, Ford, Datsun.

BOSS: Every one wrong. Come on, Tex, someone's
got to get it right.

Tex got them all in the right order. What was it?

Solution on page 117.

27. The Holdup

Officer Sharp was called to Jackson's Stationery Shop to investigate a holdup. The manager, Mr. Prince, reported that he had been held up at knifepoint and robbed of the week's receipts while his new assistant Roger was out delivering a package to a local customer.

Said Mr. Prince: "A man wearing a blue raincoat came into the shop and asked for a cheap ballpoint pen. He handed me a five-dollar bill and when I opened the cash drawer to give him his change he pulled a knife and ordered me to put all the cash into a plastic bag he took from his pocket.

"He got all the bills and most of the change when my assistant Roger came in the front door. The man pushed past me and ran through the stockroom and out the back door. I'd say he was lefthanded. He dropped the knife on his way out, and I left it where it fell in case it has fingerprints on it. I saw the man before he came into the shop. He was across the street talking to Roger."

Said Roger: "When I went out to deliver the package, a man in a blue raincoat stopped me and asked the way to Southport. I told him where to get the bus and he went off in that direction. When I got back, I heard shouting as I opened the door and saw Mr. Prince run into the stockroom. I didn't see anybody else, only Mr. Prince. Then he phoned the police and our home office."

Officer Sharp considered the two statements, took a look at the weapon, and made an arrest.

Whom did he arrest and why?

Solution on page 117.

28. Hotel Splendide

Inspector Will Ketchum was called in to investigate a series of thefts at the Hotel Splendide.

"Thanks for coming so promptly, Inspector," said the manager, as he ushered Ketchum into his office. "Recently, we've been troubled by a series of thefts from the guests' rooms, but until now we haven't been able to point a finger of suspicion at anyone."

"And now you can?" asked the Inspector. "On what grounds?"

"Yesterday a guest reported a fifty-dollar bill missing from a purse she left on the table in her room. This morning I sent one of my receptionists on an errand to the bank. In front of her at the teller was one of our chambermaids asking for change of a fifty-dollar bill. I know it doesn't prove anything, against the girl, but her pay isn't due until the end of the week, and it looks highly suspicious."

"I agree," said the Inspector. "I'd like to have a word with her, if that's possible."

"Certainly," said the manager. He pressed a button on the intercom and asked that Mabel be sent to his office. A few minutes later there was a knock on the door. A young girl entered and the manager explained why the Inspector wanted to ask her a few questions.

"It's in your interest," began the Inspector, "that you be cleared of suspicion. If it's true that you were in the bank changing a fifty-dollar bill soon after one had been stolen from a room you were working in, how did you come by that money?"

"It's true that I was in the bank with a fifty-dollar bill," admitted Mabel. "One of the guests gave it to me. I don't know which one, because it was my weekend off. When I came back yesterday—Monday—there was a telephone message for me from one of the guests who left during the weekend. I don't know who it was or where she phoned from. Lots of people come and go on weekends, and they often leave me tips."

"And you were left fifty dollars," said the Inspector. "That's quite a tip."

"Biggest I've ever had," said Mabel. "She must be rich. She left it in a funny place. I guess she wanted to be sure I got it. There's a bookcase in the lounge, full of old books I've never seen anybody read. The money was hidden in one of them on the top shelf. Myrtle, the telephone operator, took the message. Myrtle didn't get the title right, but it was by Dickens and I was supposed to look between pages 99 and 100, though she didn't say what I'd find there. There were a lot of books by Dickens to look through, and after I looked through six or seven of them and didn't find anything, I was beginning to think it was a joke."

"Do you remember which book you found it in?" asked the Inspector.

"It was *Oliver Twist*," said Mabel. "I saw the movie. Oliver asked for more, but didn't get it. I got more than I expected."

The Inspector smiled. "You may go now, Miss. Thanks for your explanation."

When the girl left, Inspector Ketchum asked the manager to call the telephone operator, Myrtle. Soon she was in the room.

"About the message you gave Mabel," the Inspector began, "how is it that you didn't know who was speaking? Why did you get only part of the message?"

"It was a really bad line," Myrtle said. "Sometimes it was clear and then it would get all noisy and crackly. I don't know where the lady was speaking from, but it may have been through a switchboard—a hotel switchboard, like ours."

"Very likely," said the Inspector.

"When the operator got through to me," continued Myrtle, "the lady must have asked her to check that we were the Hotel Splendide and was spelling it out for her. I heard the operator saying—Hotel what? Speak up, please. 'S for Samuel, yes; P for Peter, yes; L for *what*? Speak up please!' Then I chimed in and called out 'Hotel Splendide!' When the lady was put through, she asked for Mabel. I told her Mabel was off for the weekend, so she gave me a message for her to look in a book. I got as much of it as I could make sense of, what with the bad line, and other calls to deal with."

"I understand," said the Inspector. "No more questions. Thank you for your cooperation."

By the time Myrtle left, the Inspector had made his decision about the girls' stories. Have you?

Clues on page 105.
Solution on page 118.

29. The Safecrackers

The gang of safecrackers had been arrested and questioned, but the police hadn't been able to discover which ones were the three specialists. One of them specialized in picking locks and cracking combinations. One used explosives for blasting open the locks and doors. The third was an expert with drills and blowtorches. Each specialist took part only in the robberies where his or her particular skill was needed. Usually, more than one specialist took part in a robbery.

The police found out, through questioning, which gang members had taken part in each one of the last four robberies:

Steel, Trixie and Rob took part in Robbery #1, in which the lock of one safe was picked and another was blasted.

Chita, Steele, Trixie and Rocky took part in Robbery #2, in which the lock of one safe was picked and another was drilled.

Chita, Trixie, Rocky and Rob took part in Robbery #3, in which one safe was blasted and another safe had been drilled.

Chita, Steele, Trixie and Rob took part in robbery #4, in which the locks of the safes were picked, blasted and drilled.

By putting together all this information, the police finally had been able to name the lockpicker, the blaster and the driller.

Who were the three specialists?

Solution on page 118.

30. The Chess Set

Inspector Will Ketchum and Sergeant Zupp stopped outside the Olde Antique Shoppe and stared at the handsome chess set in the window. Propped up against a rook in the back row, a neatly printed card offered the set for $250.

"That set could be part of the Haley Mansion heist last week," said the Sergeant. "It fits the description of one of the two sets that was taken."

"If it is," the Inspector said, "It's worth a lot more than they're asking for it. If it's a genuine Isaak Rooker set, the kings and queens are hand carved. The only way we can be sure is to compare the kings and queens with the insurance company's photos back at the station."

"I'd be surprised if this is one of the stolen sets," said the Sergeant. "I shouldn't think it would show up so soon after the robbery —not with all the newspaper publicity it's had."

The Inspector moved closer to the window. "This could be the Tudor set that John Haley phoned us about this morning. He only just realized it had been stolen. He had lent it to his brother and found out today that his brother had returned it. So actually, three sets were stolen—not two, as the newspapers reported."

While the detectives were talking, a well-dressed elderly man went into the shop.

The Inspector caught the door before it shut. "Come on, let's go in and look around."

"That chess set in the window," the customer said to a woman who had just come out of the back room, "I noticed it last night as I was passing by. It looks like an Isaak Rooker. There are many imitations. Is this genuine?"

"Quite genuine, sir," answered the saleswoman, picking up the box the pieces were kept in. "Here, inside the lid is the maker's original label. 'Isaak Rooker.' And somebody has written on it: To Fred from Uncle Bob—Christmas 1919. And Uncle Bob has listed the pieces, too: 'Two kings—Henry VIII, two queens—Elizabeth I, four bishops, four knights—' and so on. How useful. And how nice of Uncle Bob."

"I'll take it," said the customer. The saleswoman began putting the pieces into the box.

"She's outsmarted us," whispered the Sergeant. "We have no authority to stop the sale."

"I'm taking it for granted," said the customer, "that you'll take a check."

"Certainly," said the saleswoman, "if you have identification."

The customer searched through his pockets. He had left his wallet home, he said, but he'd hurry back and get it, he was only five minutes away. He hurried out of the shop.

"We're interested in the chess set, too," Will Ketchum said to the saleswoman, "but as police officers, not customers. I know that this set could be any one of many designs by Isaak Rooker, and close comparison between the photographs and carved pieces is necessary for identification, but meanwhile, will you tell us how you came by this set?"

"I understand your curiosity, Officer," said the lady.

"Isaak Rooker chess sets were part of the Haley Mansion robbery that's been in all the papers, weren't they? I suppose you think this set is a part of it, and that somewhere on our premises we have the other two Rooker sets. You're perfectly free to search for them, if you want."

"You haven't told us yet where you got this one," said the Inspector.

"One of our customers—a man who'd visited the shop once or twice before—came in a few weeks ago with the set," said the woman. "He said he was getting rid of a few things before he went back to Australia. He came from a part of Australia where their winters are as warm as our summers—so he spends his winters there, and his summers here. He's one of the lucky ones. . . . Anyway, he took a hundred and fifty dollars for the set and seemed satisfied. If he'd come in with the set after the news of the robbery—instead of before—I'd have been suspicious. I'd have phoned the police. Anyway," she added with a smile, "John Haley isn't anyone's Uncle Bob."

The door opened and another customer came in. The saleswoman moved off to help her.

"Are we on the wrong trail?" whispered the Sergeant. "Or is this one of my off days? Does the old guy get the chess set?"

"I can give you at least three good reasons why there's a definite answer to that," said the Inspector.

Have you spotted the reasons why the customer should—or should not—be allowed to buy the chess set?

Clues on page 105.
Solution on page 119.

31. Road Blocks

The local police station received an urgent call from Waverly Mansion. It had been robbed. The robbers' car had just left and was believed to be heading for the Thruway.

The police had only two cars available, but after a quick look at their wall map, they were off at full speed to block roads at two separate points, which they knew would prevent the thieves getting to the Thruway. Which two points would they need to block?

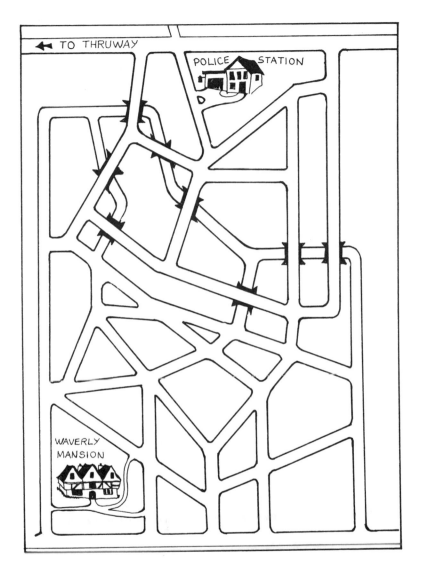

Solution on page 119.

32. Art Fake Three

Which screen is Kort Fakinnem's copy and which is the original?

Solution on page 120.

33. Open Windows at Scotland Yard

Inspector Donna DiAnsa was visiting Scotland Yard on her vacation. She watched as the police artist finished a set of drawings that pictured the chief incidents in a recent robbery.

Suddenly a gust of wind from the open window swept all the papers off the table. The Inspector helped the artist gather them together, but she laid them down on the table in the order in which they were picked up.

Can you work out the correct sequence?

Solution on page 120.

34. The Art Thieves

Six members of a gang of art thieves were rounded up, along with the proceeds of four robberies. The stolen property consisted solely of antique silver, rare books, valuable coins and old clocks.

"Judging by what these thieves stole, and what they chose to leave behind," said Inspector Donna DiAnsa, "there are four experts in the gang. One knows all about clocks; one is an authority on coins; one is a book expert; and the fourth specializes in silver."

"We know who took part in each robbery," said Sergeant Dunitz, "and we know from the articles stolen that two experts took part in each one. Here are the details," he said. He began reading this from his notebook:

Robbery #1: Coins and silver stolen. Snoz, Elvis and Ringo took part.

Robbery #2: Books and coins stolen. Drabstock, Elvis, Gertie and Ringo took part.

Robbery #3: Clocks and books stolen. Drabstock, Gertie and Fats took part.

Robbery #4: Clocks and silver stolen. Snoz, Gertie, Fats and Ringo took part.

"Good work, Sergeant," said Donna DiAnsa. "From

that we can work out who the experts are and what they went to steal."

Can you name each expert and what he or she specialized in?

Solution on page 120.

35. Three Brothers

Three brothers, Ben, Ken, and Sven had criminal records and were suspected of being responsible for three recent armed robberies. Questioning of the brothers by police, and statements by witnesses, revealed that:

1. Two of the brothers carried out the bank robbery.
2. Two of them broke into the factory.
3. Two of them raided the armored truck.
4. The one who wasn't in on the armored truck job wasn't involved in the factory break-in.
5. Sven wasn't at the factory break-in or the bank robbery.

Who did what?

Solution on page 120.

36. The Chicago Mob

A bunch of mobsters had just arrived by plane from Chicago and were waiting in one of the lounges for a car that would take them to the city.

In an adjoining lounge, separated by a glass partition, sat Inspector Will Ketchum, Sergeant Zupp and Carla Kopp, a Chicago detective who had arrived on the same plane as the mobsters.

"Take a good look at them," said Detective Kopp, "They're big trouble."

"The Sergeant here mingled with a group of them as they were waiting for their baggage," said the Inspector. He handed Carla Kopp a slip of paper. "These are the names he overheard."

Carla Kopp scanned the list. "Good work, Sergeant," she said. "You've got all seven. I'll identify them for you. I've got to be quick about it, though, because I don't want to lose them on the way to the city."

Through the glass partition, they could see the men, sitting in a row of chairs against the far wall, most of them reading magazines.

Sergeant Zupp, who was sitting with his back to the men, took out his notebook and jotted down Carla Kopp's comments as he hurriedly read through the list of names. Then Detective Kopp raced out of the room, promising fuller details later on.

"That was a bit of a rush and not easy to follow," said Inspector Ketchum. "We'd better sort it out while they're still sitting there. Read what you've got, Sergeant."

The Sergeant read from his notes:

The leader of the mob is Sly.

The one next to Sly, on his right, is Drago.

The one farthest from Drago is his brother Nolo.

The one half-way between Nolo and Drago is second in command, Vogel.

The one farthest from Vogel is Olsen, Vogel's sidekick.

The one next to Olsen is Benny.

Zeb is on Nolo's right.

"It's kind of tricky," said Inspector Ketchum. "What I want to know is which one is Sly?"

"How would you sort this out," asked Sergeant Zupp. "I can see that for anyone to be farthest from anyone else, he must be at the end. But which end?"

"Remember," hinted the Inspector, "that the end man on the right—our right as we face them—has nobody on his left. It's the opposite at the other end."

Can you work out where Sly is, and the positions of the others?

Solution on page 121.

37. Murder in the Locked Room

Inspector Keith Smilen was called to Waverly Mansion to help local police with their investigation into the death of Dudley Pinlever, the famous philanthropist. He had been found shot dead, sitting slumped over his desk in the library, a revolver close by on the floor. The police had to break open the door, because the only key to the library's only door was always kept by Pinlever personally and was found in a pocket of his jacket, which was hanging on a chair near his desk. The windows were securely locked on the inside, and though the transom over the door was unfastened, it opened no wider than about four inches. The door did not lock automatically; a key was needed to lock or unlock it.

At the time of the murder, three other people were living at Waverly Mansion. These were Norbert, the penniless playboy nephew of the wealthy Pinlever, who had come out for the weekend; James Williams, Pinlever's valet and chauffeur; and Mrs. Danvers, the housekeeper.

Sergeant Mull from the local police station met Inspector Smilen in the hall on his arrival. "Thanks for getting here so quickly, Inspector," he said. "As you know, we had Pinlever's body removed, because we were sure it was a case of suicide. The room being locked from the inside, and the only key being in Pinlever's jacket pocket, it seemed the obvious conclusion. I was here when they broke the door open, so I can fill in any missing details. Let's go into the library. Nothing has been disturbed."

"What made you suspicious?" asked the Inspector, when the Sergeant closed the library door behind them.

"Little things that came up in conversation with the housekeeper," said the Sergeant. "For example, Pinlever always liked to wear a flower in his buttonhole, and cut a fresh one himself every morning. When we broke in, the rose she saw him wearing before she went shopping at nine o'clock, was in the wastebasket. His jacket was, as you see it, hanging on the chair, but Mrs. Danvers says he usually hung it on the stand in the corner."

"What about the movements of everybody, leading up to your arrival?" asked the Inspector.

"As the housekeeper was passing the library door to go shopping, Pinlever came out and asked her to get him some cigarettes. At the time, Williams was in the garage tinkering with a noisy backfiring car. Norbert had gone for a walk and said he'd be back about noon. When the housekeeper came back, about an hour later, Williams was still in the garage, but it was quiet. She went to the library with the cigarettes, got no answer when she knocked, and Williams eventually phoned us at the station."

"Where is the nephew?"

"He hasn't returned yet. He phoned from somewhere to say he was eating out and would be back tonight. Williams is in the garage. When I saw him earlier, he was trying to remove a piece of thorn from his thumb. He said he got it while he was cutting a rose for Pinlever's buttonhole. Mrs. Danvers is annoyed at him because yesterday when Williams wanted some cotton thread to wrap around the handle of one of his tools, she lent him a full spool and he returned it with half of it gone."

"How much would that be?" asked the Inspector.

"She showed me the spool. Its full length, according to the label, was 25 yards."

"What about motive, Sergeant?" asked Inspector Smilen.

"Mrs. Danvers, none that I know of. Mr. Williams always seems to have money troubles of some sort, and once told Mrs. Danvers that Pinlever left him something in his will. The nephew is always broke and could expect to inherit everything when his uncle died."

"Do we know anything about the gun?"

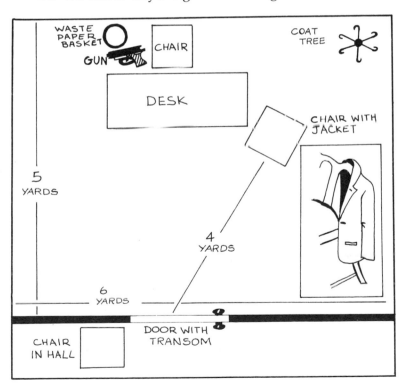

"Nothing," said the Sergeant, "we don't even know if it belonged to Pinlever." He tore a page out of his notebook and handed it to the Inspector. "I made this sketch of the scene, and I've put in a few measurements. I have a strong feeling that it's murder and Williams did it, but how he made it look like suicide I can't even guess."

"I think you're right," agreed the Inspector, studying the sketch. "As to how he made it look as if Pinlever killed himself, the rose in the wastebasket and one of these measurements give me the answer."

Do you see how he did it?

Solution on page 121.

38. The Lying Brothers

Three members of an international crime ring had been arrested and were being brought to Will Ketchum's office for questioning.

"What do we know about these three?" the Inspector asked. "Are they South American?"

"All I know about them, so far, is what Officer Tall told me before he went off duty," said Sergeant Zupp. "He understands Spanish and that's what they speak, though they seem to know some English. From what he overheard, two of them are brothers named Malo, and the other is called Bueno."

"I've heard of the Malo brothers," said the Inspector.

"I don't know which two are the brothers," continued the Sergeant, "but Officer Tall told me he'd heard the Malos agree not to give a truthful answer to any question we ask, Bueno said it was hopeless and he was going to tell the truth. I guess the Malos are going to be out to confuse us."

The Inspector had the men brought in. He asked the bald one whether his name was Bueno or Malo. The man mumbled a reply, and before the Inspector could repeat the question, the others answered.

"He says his name is Bueno," volunteered the thin one.

"He says his name is Malo," said the fat one.

The Inspector turned to Sergeant Zupp. "They're obviously keeping to their plan about who is telling the truth and who is lying. Take the brothers back to their cell and leave Bueno here with me."

Which one was Bueno: the thin one, the fat one or the bald one?

Solution on page 122.

39. Industrial Espionage

Lektron, the electronics firm, was working on a new component that they wanted to keep secret from their competitors. They had reason to believe that someone broke into their drafting office, and that the plans for the component had been stolen. Their chief draftsman, Mr. Tracer, was suspicious enough to call in the police.

The drafting office, on the third floor of an office building, had been locked up on Saturday noon for the weekend, but on Monday the staff returned to find the transom of the office door broken. The door was still locked and the blueprint of the component was spread flat on the desk.

"I knew I should have put it in the safe," said Mr. Tracer, as Inspector Donna DiAnsa looked around the office. "It looks as if somebody broke the glass, opened the transom and climbed through. The window cleaner is supposed to have broken it accidentally."

"So I understand," said the Inspector. "You say nothing has been stolen. Was there any glass on the blueprint?"

"There were a few splinters of glass on top of it," said Mr. Tracer, lifting the blueprint, "and these small fragments underneath it."

Donna DiAnsa studied the fragments. "You have good reason to be suspicious. Have you spoken to the building management?"

"I spoke to the manager in his office before I phoned the police," said Mr. Tracer.

"I've already had a word with him myself," said the Inspector. "He's arranging for me to interview the three people who were on the premises Saturday afternoon: the janitor, the window cleaner—the one who cleans the transoms and the windows on the landings on Saturday afternoons—and a locksmith who was called in to change a couple of locks for new tenants."

"The janitor has been fairly helpful," said Mr. Tracer. "He has that cubbyhole sort of office in the hall and he's also the doorkeeper, porter, supervisor of the maintenance people and just about everything else."

"I've met him," said the Inspector. "The offices on the lower floors are rented mostly to lawyers and insurance agents, and the office doors are numbered 1 to 70. On this floor are the bigger, more permanent tenants, on these doors you have your names instead of numbers."

The telephone rang. It was the manager of the building with a message for Donna DiAnsa, telling her the three men were now waiting in a room next to the manager's office.

"Before you question them," said the manager, when the Inspector arrived, "I have some details here that may be helpful. It's a rough timetable of Saturday's comings and goings, supplied mostly by our janitor." From a slip of paper he read out:

1:00 P.M. Sam Shammy, the window cleaner, arrives, starts work.

1:05 P.M. Lem Lever, the locksmith, arrives to change the locks.

1:35 P.M. Lever leaves the premises to get a special file.

1:00 P.M. Sam Shammy, the window cleaner, arrives, starts work.

1:05 P.M. Lem Lever, the locksmith, arrives to change the locks.

1:35 P.M. Lever leaves the premises to get a special file.

2:00 P.M. Shammy has fall. Breaks Lektron's transom.

2:05 P.M. Lever returns with special file.

2:10 P.M. Shammy returns limping to janitor's office.

2:15 P.M. Shammy cannot work, goes home.

2:20 P.M. Janitor at Lektron. Removes loose glass from transom.

"Very useful," commented the Inspector. "Ask the janitor to come in, please."

"When Mr. Lever left to get the file," said Donna DiAnsa to the janitor, "did he take his tool box with him?"

"No," said the janitor, "he left it in my office. He left his coat, too, and hurried off with his jacket all unbuttoned. He's usually a very neat guy."

"Did you find Lektron's transom unfastened when you climbed the ladder to remove the loose glass?" asked the Inspector. "And could you see whether there was anything on the desk just below you? I mean, the desk standing against the wall, just clear of the door."

"The transom was fastened," said the janitor. "There was a blueprint on the desk—I'd say, it measured about one foot by three feet. I didn't notice any details. I was too busy with the glass. When I removed the loose pieces, I tried tapping the rest of it loose, but it was breaking and scattering inside the office, so I decided to leave it and finish the job when the staff got in and I could work from the inside."

The Inspector thanked the janitor for his help and asked to see the window cleaner next.

Sam Shammy limped in, and Donna DiAnsa asked about his fall.

"The ladder slipped as I was coming down," explained Mr. Shammy. "It swung around and threw me off, and the top end shattered the transom. I didn't see anything lying around in the office. There was definitely nothing on the desk. And ask the locksmith what he was doing on that floor, where he had no business being."

When Lem Lever, the locksmith, was brought in, the Inspector asked if he had been on the third floor.

"I was," he admitted, "because of the room numbers stamped on the little metal disc attached to the keys. I've only been here once before and I never got used to which way to hold the disc—six upside down looks like nine—sixteen looks like 91 and 66 looks like 99."

"There isn't a 91 or a 99," said the Inspector. "Seventy is the highest room number."

"I know that now," said Lever, "but I didn't know it then. I was given two keys—24 was one. No problem. Sixty-nine was the other. Ninety-six was how I saw it. And when I couldn't find anything higher than 70 on the second floor, I went up to the third. No numbers at all up there. So I knocked, thought I'd ask. But nobody answered. So I went down to get on with the job at 24. Then I realized my mistake and did both jobs."

"An easy mistake to make," said the Inspector, dismissing him. "Thanks for your explanation."

At Donna DiAnsa's request, Mr. Tracer was phoned and asked to come down to the manager's office.

"Sit down, Mr. Tracer," said the manager. "Inspector DiAnsa has some news for you."

"I'm afraid your secret component is no longer a secret," said the Inspector. "The damage is done. I'm going into the next room to make an arrest. But there's still time to prevent anyone else patenting your idea before you do."

Who is going to be arrested—and why?

And can you deduce why the secret is out?

Clue on page 105.
Solution on page 122.

40. Duke's Gang

Sergeant Zupp tapped on the door of Will Ketchum's office. "Just had a phone call from Stan Boskin," he said, placing a piece of paper on the desk. "This is the same Stan Boskin who was once a member of the Duke Gang. He says three of the top boys have just arrived at the Gaslight Club and are about to leave for a high level meeting and will take different routes and be in disguise."

"Which three?" asked Inspector Ketchum, picking up the piece of paper.

"He said it was Duke, Robby and Midge," said the Sergeant. "And the cars they're driving—a Ferrari, a Porsche and a Mercedes—are parked side by side. Stan hung up all of a sudden while I was trying to get the details down. It would have been useful to know who was driving which car. Maybe he'll call back."

The Inspector studied the four brief statements the Sergeant had extracted from Stan Boskin's rambling conversation. With a puzzled frown, he read them out:

Robby's car is parked next to the Porsche.
The Mercedes is parked next to Duke's car.
Robby used to own the Mercedes.
Midge's tie is the same color as the Ferrari.

The Inspector's face suddenly lit up. "You don't have to call Stan back," he said. "This tells me who is driving each car."

Does it tell you?

Solution on page 123.

41. Dope Ring

The Chief of the Narcotics Squad studied the photo of the three men who were leaning against the ship's railing.

"What do we know about these characters?" he asked.

"Not much," his assistant answered. "One of them is from Denmark, one from Germany and the other from Sweden. They've been operating a dope ring in Brussels, but now they're probably in the States. The only information that came with this photo is that one of these guys is the supplier, one is a pusher, and the other acts as a courier between the two."

"Which is which in the photo?"

"All we've been told," said the assistant, "is that the Dane is to the left of the Swede; the courier is to the right of the supplier; the pusher is to the left of the German, and the German is to the left of the Swede. When they say to the left of—or to the right of—they don't necessarily mean next to. And left or right means as we're looking at the photo, not the person's left or right."

"They haven't told us much," said the Chief, "but it should be enough to work out which is which."

Is it enough for you?

Solution on page 123.

42. Art Fake Four

Which picture is Kort Fakinnem's copy and which is the original?

Solution on page 124.

43. The Clickspring Cup

It was the town's turn to stage the annual garden show. Exhibitors from all the surrounding towns were competing for the silver cups and for the famous Clickspring Gold Cup, donated by wealthy socialite Harold Clickspring, and awarded to the best exhibitor.

Today was the big day. Then an hour before Clickspring was due to make the presentation, the Clickspring Gold Cup was stolen right from under the nose of the plainsclothes policeman who was guarding it.

"It's a mystery," said Sergeant Mull to his old friend, Inspector Will Ketchum, who was spending his vacation at the local hotel with his hound Sherlock. "I'm glad you're here. Your unofficial help will be very welcome. I was against putting the prizes on display. The tent in which they put them is too close to the fence for good security. It's a wilderness on the other side."

"I agree," said Inspector Ketchum. "Any witnesses?"

"According to Officer Sharp, who was on duty when the theft of the cup was discovered, there were three people present at the only time it could have happened. The cups were displayed on a table at the far end of the tent. There were ten silver cups. The gold one stood on a small box in front of the others. They're all small cups—about five inches high. The gold one was a little taller. It's insured for $5000."

"Was anyone else in the tent besides the three witnesses?" asked Will Ketchum.

"Lots of people," said Sergeant Mull, "but not near the prize table. The middle of the tent is clear from the entrance to the prize table, but all around the sides are stands selling fruit, flowers, vegetables and gardening aids of all kinds. Two of the witnesses are waiting for me in the officials' tent now. The other one went off into the crowd. Officer Sharp is looking for him."

"I'll help if I can," said Will Ketchum. "Tell me what you know so far."

Around the time of the theft, the Sergeant explained, there were three young men looking at the display. They didn't seem to be together. One was carrying a bundle of about a dozen thin garden canes. The second looked like a hiker, and had a small knapsack on his back. The third was wearing shorts and carrying a cauliflower in a string bag which he had evidently bought at one of the stands. When the first one turned to go, his garden canes poked into the display, knocking the cups off the table and onto the ground. In the few seconds it took to pick up the cups, the gold one had disappeared.

"What about the knapsack?" asked Will Ketchum.

"None of them objected to being searched," answered the Sergeant. "When Officer Sharp reported to me and said he'd let the three of them go, I sent him back to find them."

Just then Officer Sharp came up to report that all three men were waiting. After a few more questions from Will Ketchum, they went into the officials' tent to speak with them.

Officer Sharp introduced the three witnesses as Wynn Wheeler, a cyclist on his way to visit relatives at Saybrook; Wes Walker, a hiker; and Fred Flyer from a nearby town.

"If you were on your way to Saybrook, Mr. Wheeler," said Sergeant Mull, "why did you come this way? And why did you buy a cauliflower?"

"I wanted to be at my aunt's in Saybrook in time for supper," explained Wheeler. "I stopped for a cool drink at the Bikers' Cafe in Hillsdale, and when I came out I found that somebody had stolen my bike light, my pump and even the pennant off my handlebars. I went to the police station there and reported it. You can check that out with them. Coming through these grounds is a shortcut, even with the fence to climb over."

"Hillsdale is only four miles from here," said the Sergeant. "You should have passed through here long before now."

"I had trouble halfway between Hillsdale and here," Wheeler said. "Near Comstock Farm I had a puncture. Not a soul in sight, but luckily my puncture repair outfit was still in my saddlebag. It delayed me half an hour, though, and I couldn't make up the time, so I came this way."

"What about the cauliflower?" asked Sergeant Mull.

"I was pushing my bike past that tent, and I looked in," answered Wheeler. "When I saw all those vegetables, I thought I'd bring something for my aunt. I propped my bike against the fence and went and bought a cauliflower and a string bag. Then I saw the cups and went to have a look. While I was standing there, somebody accidentally knocked some cups off the table. I helped to pick them up, and for my trouble got suspected of stealing one. I started out again, but figured the bulky vegetable was a nuisance, so I gave it away to an old lady. Now here I am and still getting nowhere."

"Thanks for your explanation, Mr. Wheeler," said the Sergeant. "Now, Mr. Flyer, you said you were in the tent buying canes for kite-making. Aren't the garden canes kind of heavy for kites?"

"Maybe you're right," said Fred Flyer. "They're for a double box-kite. I never made one before, but you don't succeed if you don't try, do you? If you're going to ask me what happened at the prize table, I had the canes under my arm and somehow they knocked off the cups. I helped fix up the table, and got searched for my trouble, too."

"And you, Mr. Walker," the Sergeant went on, "you allowed Officer Sharp to search you and your knapsack, and although you say you're on a hiking trip, you don't seem to be carrying a map."

"I had one until a few hours ago," said Mr. Walker. "I saw the posters advertising this show, so I came over to see it. On my way here I stopped on the river bridge to watch some boys playing on a raft. I leaned against the parapet, watching them until they drifted out of sight around a bend. I never noticed my map slipping out of my shirt pocket. It floated down under the bridge. I ran to the river bank, hoping it would be within reach, but it already sank. I've got to buy a new one. I don't know how the accident in the tent happened."

Will Ketchum took Sergeant Mull aside and whispered that he suggested letting them all go. He was sure that if the two who lied were closely watched, the gold cup would be recovered.

Which two lied, and why should they be watched?

Solution on page 124.

Clues

1. Three's Company at the Greasy Spoon—Since all the identities were guessed wrong, that reduces each name to only two possibilities. Slick is reduced to only one, because he was spoken to by the man with the mustache, so he couldn't be that one.

3. The Sneak Thief—There is a clue in each of the following statements:

1. "My briefcase was locked."
2. "I got to town this morning just before noon on one of those one-day round-trip excursion tickets—"
3. "I was hoping to find some secondhand books."
4. "All I had to spend since I got off the train this morning was what they charged me at the checkroom."

4. Odd Man Out—You'll find clues in the following items:

1. the dogs' collars
2. that hat
3. the jackets (don't forget that the buttoning of men's clothing is the opposite of women's)
4. the newspapers

5. Doggone Kids—Note which boys were not present each time the dogs were seen, and go on from there.

7. Counterfeiting Ring—Look again at what the suspects have to say.

8. Ditched!—If the hitchhiker, the blonde and Pam were the three people sitting together, they would have been on the back seat. Jim, Ben, Ann and the girl with the brown hair couldn't have been four people sitting together, but must have been at least three.

9. Lying in the Gym—Eliminate each boy about whom more than one statement would be true if he were guilty.

11. The Crypto Caper—The second word is obviously a day of the week: and since it's six letters long it must be Sunday, Monday or Friday. Therefore, 342 must be SUN, MON or FRI. It can't be FRI, because 2 would then be I and that would make the first word of the message OI which isn't an English word. So 2 is N, and the day is Sunday or Monday.

12. Down at the Dirty Duck—The Frenchman has the Englishman on his left, so the Australian . . .

13. Alibis—Look at the money spent and at the seating arrangements.

14. Post Office—From Statement #1 you can deduce that the gunman could be the short one; the lookout could be the tall one, and either man could be the medium one. Where the statements indicate that a man is taller than one—and shorter than the other—that statement tells you something about each one of the three men.

16. The Coin Expert—Look again at the coin expert's name, the young man's relationship to him, and the date of the coin.

22. The Clickspring Caper—Consider the view from the gate, and from the broken window. Also give some thought to the broken glass and the footprints.

28. Hotel Splendide—Consider again where Mabel said she found the fifty-dollar bill, and also the point just before Myrtle chimed in between the other operator and the caller.

30. The Chess Set—Consider the Sergeant's first mention of the stolen sets, John Haley's comments, and the saleswoman's reference to "the other two Rooker sets." Look again at what Uncle Bob wrote in the box lid. Consider the comings and goings of the Australian.

39. Industrial Espionage—Think about the numbers on the keys, and also where Mr. Tracer found the scattered glass fragments.

Solutions

1. Three's Company at the Greasy Spoon—Slick was smoking; Mug was wearing the hat; Smiley had the mustache.

Slick, wrongly guessed by the detective as the man wearing the hat, was spoken to by the one with the mustache, so he couldn't be either of them. Therefore he must be the man smoking the cigar.

Mug was wrongly guessed to be the one with the mustache, and since Slick is the smoker, Mug must be the one in the hat.

Smiley is, therefore, the one with the mustache.

2. Art Fake—The second picture is the fake.

The book has its title on the back cover.

The subject has a glove on his right hand, but the glove on the ground is also a right-hand glove.

3. The Sneak Thief—The contents of the suspect's pockets do not include:

1. A key to the briefcase
2. The "return" part of the ticket
3. Enough cash (and no other way of paying) for buying books

Mr. Fink was arrested and charged. It was easy to find the owner of the briefcase. It turned out that he had put his case down while buying a newspaper, and in a matter of seconds it had disappeared. The sneak thief had rehearsed his story well, in case he was questioned, but he hadn't allowed for the contents of his pockets giving him away.

4. Odd Man Out—One of the dogs must be wearing a collar, because one of the fathers (A) has a leash in his hand. The white dog clearly has no collar, so the black dog must belong to Family A.

One of the mothers is without a jacket, and the jacket carried by Father A is a lady's jacket (it has buttons on the left-hand side), so it must be his wife's jacket. He therefore, and the jacketless mother, and the black dog all belong to Family A.

One of the girls is wearing ribbons in her hair, so she isn't likely to have a hat, too. Therefore the girl without the hair ribbons belongs to the mother carrying the child's hat (Mother A).

The man and woman (Mother B) who have bought identical copies of a newspaper are not likely to be together, so he is the suspected pickpocket, and the rest belong to Family B.

5. Doggone Kids—The pairs are: Red—boxer
Scruffy—Irish setter
Shorty—the pug
Curly—the collie

The boxer and the pug were seen with Shorty and Red, so neither dog belongs to Scruffy or Curly.

Shorty and Curly were seen with the pug and the collie, and since the pug doesn't belong to Curly, it must belong to Shorty.

Therefore, the boxer belongs to Red and the collie must belong to Curly.

Scruffy and Curly were seen with the collie and the Irish setter, so the Irish setter belongs to Scruffy.

6. Meanwhile Back at the Hideout . . .—Order: 3—2—6—1—4—5

All the loot is now hidden in the safe place the money from the bank used to occupy down the well on Elm Farm. Every gang member is to go there by car and travel alone.

7. Counterfeiting Ring—The one who lied was Mr. Brush.

If, as he said, he had received four one-dollar bills as change from the five-dollar bill he handed to the cab-driver, the fare would have been $1 or less. If it had been, he would have paid with the one-dollar bill, especially since he wanted to keep the five-dollar bill because of the phone number he'd written on it. No matter how he paid his fare, the story he made up to explain his possession of the counterfeit bills shows he is lying.

8. Ditched!—Pam was driving.

If the hitchhiker, the blonde and Pam were the three sitting together, they would have to occupy the back seat, but since the other group sitting together consisted of at least three people—Jim, Ben and Ann/the girl with the brown hair—these must have been the ones sitting in the back. Ann and the girl with brown hair must be the same person: otherwise four people would have been in the back seat.

So Pam must be the blonde girl. Therefore, Pam and the hitchhiker were sitting in the front seat.

Since the hitchhiker wouldn't have been driving, Pam must have been the driver.

9. Lying in the Gym—Tim.

He was the only boy about whom just one truthful statement was made (by Dan). Had any other of the four boys been the guilty one, and the same statements been made, more than one boy would have been telling the truth. But only one boy was telling the truth, as stated by the principal.

10. Cracked!—Potsy shot both "Legs" and "Ears."

The hole nearest the door handle was the first, because none of its cracks were stopped by any other. The hole farthest from the door handle was the second, because its cracks are stopped only by the cracks from the first. The middle hole is the last, because its cracks are stopped by the cracks of both the others.

11. The Crypto Caper—The message reads: On Sunday at six get the gang together at the Juniper Tree Inn to plan our next big job.

In the window, the farthest hole from the door was the first, since it has no stopped cracks. The one nearest the door was the second, since it was stopped only by the first. The one next to the second was the third, since it was stopped only by the previous two. The remaining one, stopped by all the others, was the fourth.

12. Down at the Dirty Duck—The Frenchman.

As Eddie has the Australian on his right, Eddie must be one of the other two. He cannot be the Englishman, because the Australian, not the Frenchman, would be on his right. So Eddie must be the Frenchman.

13. Alibis—Jack Cass and Deke.

All three men may have been involved in the factory job, but Jack's and Deke's alibis had not been well enough thought out to fool Ketchum.

Jack Cass could not have paid exactly $100 for the tickets, because that amount is not divisible by three.

Deke could not have been sitting next to the kid and two parents, because on that side of him there were only two seats—numbers 1 and 2, and on the other side of him were the three elderly ladies.

14. Post Office—Gunman—Tim, short, redheaded
Lookout—Jim, medium, dark-haired
Driver—Mush, tall, blond.

Statement #1 says that the gunman is shorter than the lookout, so the gunman must be either the short or the medium one, and the lookout is either the medium or the tall one.

Statements #2 and #3 say Jim is shorter than one man (the driver) and taller than the other (the redhead), so Jim must be medium.

Since Jim is medium, the driver must be the tall one, and the redhead must be the short one.

Since the driver is the tall one, the lookout (medium or tall in Statement #1) *must* be medium, and the gunman (short or medium in Statement #1) *must* be the short one, as well as the redhead.

Statement #4 says Mush is taller than the dark-haired one. The dark-haired one, therefore can't be the tall one, and is not the redheaded short one (Statement #3), so he must be the medium one (Jim).

Mush then is the tall one, with blond hair.

15. Under Surveillance—9—11—1—8—5—7—3—10—2—12—6—4.

16. The Coin Expert—Donna DIAnsa tested the young man by referring to Mr. Silver as his Uncle "George," which the man didn't question, although, being "C. J." Silver, he was obviously not a George.

Mr. Silver, being an only child and a lifelong bachelor, could not be anybody's uncle.

No coin could be given a BC (Before Christ) date, because nobody knew beforehand how many years later

Christ would be born, which showed that the young man had not asked Mr. Silver, who would certainly have known.

17. More Doggone Kids—The pairs are:
Skinny—cocker spaniel
Freckles—poodle
Braids—German shepherd
Red—no dog.
On Monday all but the cocker spaniel and Skinny were seen together, so those two must be dog and owner.

On Friday, all but the white dog and Freckles were seen together, so they are dog and owner.

Next, Freckles and her dog were seen with Red, so Red is not a dog owner. The remaining pair, therefore, are the German shepherd and Braids.

18. Cliff Tragedy—If a rope is cut while it's under strain, it frays during the cutting, particularly the last few strands. And, if the rope had been attached to the victim when he fell, it would have followed him down and landed on top of him. The rope, however, was found *underneath* the victim, and the rope ends were not frayed.

The Inspector's theory was that, during a struggle on the top of the cliff, John Fell had either been pushed over the edge or had fallen over accidentally, and a cover story was made up about the rope. The rope had been cut with a knife, and a length was taken down to the beach and mistakenly pushed underneath Fell's body instead of being tied around his waist. Harry and Peter were detained for questioning.

19. The Protection Racket—Mr. North operates in the South.
Mr. South operates in the East.
Mr. East operates in the West.

Mr. West operates in the North.

Since Mr. East's area is not East, North or South, it must be West.

Since Mr. South's area cannot also be West, and it's not South or North, it must be East.

Mr. North's area cannot be West or East, and it is not North, so it must be South.

Mr. West's area must be the only remaining area—North.

20. The Braney Safe—Four-dial: LYNX and MOLE (or MOLE and LYNX).

Five-dial: When the middle dial is turned one place right or left, the top and bottom letters read as "I." When a Z is turned from a side position to top or bottom, it becomes an "N." Then the first dial from the left is turned one place to the left (O), and the next is turned one place to the right (N), the middle one to the left (I) and the next to the right (O) and the last to the left (N), the top letters read ONION. So do the bottom letters, in reverse.

21. The Card Players—Clockwise the players are: Fingers, Doc, Spider, Kinky.

Since Kinky is not opposite Fingers, he must be either to the left or right of him.

Since Kinky is (according to Stu) on Spider's left, Spider must be opposite Fingers (because if Spider were to the left or right of Fingers, Kinky would either have to be in Finger's place or opposite him, which Stu said he was not).

So, since Spider is opposite Fingers, and Kinky is left of Spider, Doc must be in the remaining place, opposite Kinky.

22. The Clickspring Caper—Tom Bean and Mr. Paley.

Tom Bean said he saw the open window from the

gate. Later he said he couldn't see the gate from the window because of the trees. If he could see the window from the gate, he should have been able to see the gate from the window. So he lied.

If the window had been broken by anybody standing where the footprints were, and the glass had fallen around his feet, none would have fallen *under* his feet and gotten pressed into the earth. Moreover, the broken glass would have fallen inside (not outside) the room, if the window had been broken from the outside. So, if the window was broken from the inside, and Mr. Paley was the only person (apart from the police) with a key, he must have been involved in the plan that went wrong.

Paley's part in the plan soon came out. He filled a sack with the goods he was stealing and left it in the hall. Next he broke the window from the inside and opened it. Then, leaving the front door unfastened, he went outside and made the footprints with an old pair of Clickspring's boots. Finally, he went to the village inn.

Soon afterward, Tom Bean arrived at the gate, went straight to the front door (which was still open), took the sack from the hall and left, making for the woods. Unfortunately for him, Officer Luke Sharp was passing the gate at that moment.

23. Art Fake Two—The second picture is the fake.

The A-branding iron on the ground would brand an A, but the other would not brand a Z as the sheep is branded. The Z would be the wrong way around.

24. The Forgers—Left—Dick, the printer.
Middle—Tom the engraver.
Right—Harry the distributor.

Since Harry is not next to the printer, he must occupy one of the trucks on the end—right or left (otherwise, he'd surely be next to the printer).

If Harry is to the right of Tom, he must be on the right side.

That puts Tom in the middle, and the only place left for Dick is on the left.

Since the printer is not next to Harry, he can't be in the middle, so he must be on the left. It follows that if Dick is on the left, Dick is the printer.

Since the engraver (and Tom) is next to Dick, Tom is the engraver. Harry, therefore, is the distributor.

25. Crypto Strikes Again—The message read: After the Wilton Parade Jewelry Shop job, the share out will be at the Five Jolly Sailors Tavern. Tell Nutty and Al to be there.

26. The Bank Robbery—Ford, Datsun, Chevy, Toyota.

Mutt was all wrong, so Lem's placing of the Chevy and Ford (being the same as Mutt's) must also have been wrong. But Lem had two right, so these must have been the Datsun (second) and the Toyota (fourth).

Clem had only one right: it wasn't the Toyota, because Mutt had that second and Mutt was all wrong. It wasn't the Datsun, because we already know that was one of the ones that Lem had correct as #2. And it wasn't the Chevy, which he named fourth, because Lem was correct about the Toyota being #4. So it had to be Ford, which he named as #1.

This leaves the third place to the Chevy.

27. The Holdup—The knife could not have fallen so close behind the door without being pushed away when the door was opened. So Mr. Prince was lying. He had robbed the cash drawer himself, and to divert suspicion, made up the story of the holdup, which included the stranger he had seen talking to Roger. His careless placing of the knife was his downfall and led to his arrest.

The visible hinges on the stockroom door showed Luke Sharp that the door opened inwards.

28. Hotel Splendide—The girls chose the wrong page numbers between which the fifty-dollar bill was to be found, because they were impossible. Pages 99 and 100 are the front and back of the same page. Mabel said she looked between these pages in several books until she eventually found the bill.

Myrtle, the telephone operator, could not have received the message she repeated. She too must have been lying when she said that the other operator, repeating the letters called back "S for Samuel, P for Peter, L for what?" Since she knew the letter was L, there was no reason to ask what it stood for.

Mabel, knowing she had been seen in the bank breaking the fifty-dollar bill soon after it had been reported stolen, evidently invented a cover story with Myrtle's help.

29. The Safecrackers—The specialists were:
Rob—blaster
Steele—lockpicker
Chita—driller

In Robbery #1, neither Steele nor Trixie could have been the blaster, because they were both at Robbery #2, where there was no blaster. So Rob must be the blaster, and either Steele or Trixie is the lockpicker.

In Robbery #2, since Steele or Trixie is the lockpicker, Chita or Rocky must be the driller.

In Robbery #4, Chita must be the driller, because Rocky, the other possibility, was not there.

In Robbery #3, since Rob is the blaster and Chita is the driller, Trixie and Rocky cannot be specialists.

In Robbery #4, since Trixie is not a specialist and Chita is the driller and Rob the blaster, Steele must be the lockpicker.

30. The Chess Set—The newspaper reports mentioned, as stated by Sergeant Zupp, only two chess sets stolen. The saleswoman mentioned "the other two sets." Only John Haley, the police and the thieves knew at this point that three sets had been stolen.

Uncle Bob's writing on the box-lid label must have been a forgery, because in 1919, the first Queen Elizabeth did not have a number. It wasn't until later, when there was a second Queen Elizabeth, that a number became necessary. The original label in the box must have included some telltale information that it was better to cover than to remove.

The tale about the Australian must have been invented, because it is not possible to follow an Australian winter with a European summer. They take place at the same time.

31. Road Blocks—The police cars leave the station, cross the five-road junction and go over the bridge. At the T-junction, one turns right and goes over the bridge, turning left at the end and stopping there. The other turns left, goes over the bridge, turns right into the next road and stops there. (See below.)

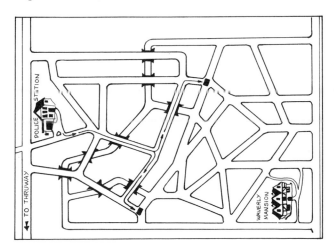

32. Art Fake Three—The first screen is the fake.

The three signatures are exactly the same and are obviously three copies of one signature. Even only two signatures by the same person are rarely exactly the same.

Also when Kort added the moon, he forgot to change the direction of the shadow of the telephone pole.

33. Open Windows at Scotland Yard—10—5—12—8—9—1—6—3—4—11—2—7.

34. The Art Thieves—The four experts are:
Elvis—coins
Snoz—silver
Drabstock—books
Fats—clocks

In Robberies #1 and #2, in which coins were stolen, only Elvis and Ringo were at both. But Ringo was also at Robbery #4, where no coins were stolen, so Elvis must be the coin expert.

Therefore, since Elvis wasn't the silver thief at Robbery #1, it must have been either Snoz or Ringo. Ringo however was at Robbery #2, where no silver was stolen, so the silver expert must be Snoz. The experts at Robbery #1 were Elvis and Snoz, so Ringo was not an expert.

In Robbery #2 Elvis was the coin expert and Ringo was not an expert, so the book expert was either Drabstock or Gertie. But Gertie was at Robbery #4, where no books were stolen. So Drabstock must be the book expert and Gertie is not an expert.

In Robbery #3, since Drabstock was the book expert and Gertie was not an expert, the clock expert must be Fats.

35. Three Brothers—According to Statement #4, the same two brothers were involved in the armored truck job and the factory break-in. Sven was not at the factory break-in, so he was not at the armored truck job, and since he was not at the bank robbery, he took part in none of the robberies. Ben and Ken therefore committed all three.

36. The Chicago Mob—The order from the left was: Olsen, Benny, Drago, Sly, Vogel, Zeb, Nolo.

Nolo was the farthest from Drago, and Olsen was the farthest from Vogel. The farthest a man can be from another is at the end of the row, and the man he is farthest from must be farther from him than the middle. So Nolo and Olsen are end men, and Drago and Vogel are next to either the middle man or an end man.

The end man on the right of the row (as viewed from the front) has a man on his right only, and the other end man has someone on his left only. Zeb was on Nolo's right, so Nolo was the right end man, Olsen the left end man. Benny was next to Olsen, so Drago (farther from Nolo than the middle man) must have been next to Benny, and Vogel (farther from Olsen than the middle man) must have been next to Zeb. Sly was in the remaining middle position.

37. Murder in the Locked Room Pinlever, according to Mrs. Danvers, cut the rose for his buttonhole himself, so Williams was evidently lying when he said he got the thorn in his thumb cutting the rose.

Inspector Smilen deduced that Williams shot Pinlever soon after Mrs. Danvers left to go shopping. He arranged the backfiring of the car's engine as a cover for the revolver shot. He got Pinlever to open the door for him, shot him and then took the key from Pinlever's pocket, carefully positioning the chair and jacket. He removed the rose from Pinlever's buttonhole (getting a thorn in his thumb). Then he took Mrs. Danvers' thread, and cut off more than enough to go twice the distance from the jacket to the transom. He threaded one end through the buttonhole and drew the two ends through the open transom, holding them with one hand while he closed and locked the door with the other. Standing on the hall chair which he had already placed in position, he led the thread through the ring of the key, pulled the sag out of it, and slid the key down the lower half of the thread to the jacket. Keeping the upper thread tight, and allowing the lower one to sag, he managed to get the key to drop into the pocket of Pinlever's jacket. When the key was deep in the pocket, Williams let the lower thread go and carefully drew the upper thread through the buttonhole until he recovered the whole length of thread through the transom.

Williams later admitted his guilt.

38. The Lying Brothers—The thin one.

The bald man's mumbled answer must have been "Bueno," whether he was a truthful Bueno or a lying Malo. Therefore, since the thin one said the mumbled answer was "Bueno," he *must have been* the truthful Bueno, because if he had been a lying Malo, he would have said that the mumbled answer was "Malo."

39. Industrial Espionage—Donna DiAnsa arrested Lem Lever, the locksmith.

The statements made by the window cleaner and the janitor (about the shattering of the transom and the removing of the broken glass, both of which caused the scattering of glass fragments) agreed with Mr. Tracer's testimony that he found glass fragments on the blueprint and underneath it. This told Donna DiAnsa that the blueprint was not on the desk when the transom was shattered at 2:00 P.M. while the locksmith was out of the building. But it was back on the desk when the janitor started removing the broken glass at 2:20 P.M., after the locksmith returned.

The locksmith lied when he gave his reason for being on the wrong floor, because the number 69 on the room-key disc—when seen upside down—would still be 69, not 96!

According to the statement made by the locksmith after his arrest, the president of a rival electronics company for whom Lem worked occasionally knew that he sometimes did jobs in Lektron's office building. He offered Lem money to get into Lektron's drafting office and "borrow" any drawings he could find. They would be copied immediately while Lem waited, and he could then return them.

To get the blueprint out of the building and back in again without the theft being noticed, Lem rolled it up and pushed it up his jacket sleeve. Because he was a locksmith, picking Lektron's lock was no problem at all for him.

40. Duke's Gang—Midge owns the Mercedes, Robby owns the Ferrari and Duke owns the Porsche.

Since Robby's car is parked next to the Porsche, and he *used* to own the Mercedes, he must own the Ferrari now.

The Mercedes is parked *next to* Duke's car, so it can't belong to him. The Ferrari doesn't belong to Duke either, because we know that it's Robby's; therefore the Porsche must be Duke's.

That leaves Midge with the Ferrari. The information that Midge's tie is the same color as the Ferrari is of no use at all.

41. Dope Ring—Dane—the pusher
German—the supplier
Swede—the courier
Since the Dane and the German are to the left of the Swede, the Swede must be on the extreme right. Since

the pusher is to the left of the German, the pusher must be the Dane.

The German, therefore, must be the one in the middle. Since the pusher is on the extreme left, and the courier is on the right of the supplier, the courier must be on the extreme right, and the supplier in the middle.

42. Art Fake Four—The first picture is the fake.
EMKort added the weathervane which, like all weathervanes, should point into the wind. Here it shows the wind direction to the opposite of that shown by the smoke coming from the chimneys.

43. The Clickspring Cup—Wynn Wheeler and Wes Walker lied.

Wynn Wheeler could have mended his puncture, but he could not have inflated the tire without the pump that he said had been stolen. And at a place where there was "not a soul in sight" nobody could have helped him.

Wes Walker could have watched a raft drifting out of sight around a bend, but as the river would be flowing in that direction, his fallen map would have floated in the same direction—away from the bridge, not under it—as he stated.

There were no contradictions in Fred Flyer's statement.

Wynn Wheeler and Wes Walker were watched, and they led police to the gold cup in time for the presentation. It turned out that the two men had seen posters that mentioned the gold cup and had worked out a plan to steal it. At first, the knapsack was part of the plan, but the sight of the vegetables on sale in the tent inspired a quick change to a better plan. They bought a large cauliflower and, in secret, cut off one end of it in a wedge shape so that it would stay in position when replaced. After scraping out the insides of the cauliflower, they returned to the tent, with the string bag wrapped around the outside of the cauliflower. Then they waited for the right moment to distract the attention of the guard and pop the cup into the cauliflower. They slid the vegetable into the string bag, where it looked as though it had been all the while, and then Wynn Wheeler went off and hid the cup away for them to fetch later. They were caught in the act of collecting it.

Index